THE PURPOSE PITCH

THE PURPOSE PITCH

KATHRYN MOCKLER

MANSFIELD PRESS

a stuart ross book

Printed in Canada

Library and Archives Canada Cataloguing in Publication

Mockler, Kathryn, 1971-, author
The purpose pitch / Kathryn Mockler.

Poems.
ISBN 978-1-77126-069-5 (pbk.)

I. Title.

PS8626.O35P87 2015 C811'.6 C2015-901398-4

Editor: Stuart Ross
Typesetting & cover design: Stuart Ross
Cover art: David Poolman, *The Civil War*, graphite & hydrocal, 2015

The publication of *The Purpose Pitch* has been generously supported by the Canada Council for the Arts and the Ontario Arts Council

ONTARIO ARTS COUNCIL
CONSEIL DES ARTS DE L'ONTARIO
an Ontario government agency
un organisme du gouvernement de l'Ontario

Canada Council for the Arts Conseil des arts du Canada

Mansfield Press Inc.
25 Mansfield Avenue, Toronto, Ontario, Canada M6J 2A9
Publisher Denis De Klerck
www.mansfieldpress.net

CONTENTS

SEALED CONTAINERS

—So how are we going to get out of here?

—Why do you repeat my questions?

—I don't repeat your questions.

—You repeated my question about getting out of here.

—We need a plan.

—I can't think of anything.

—Let's think of three ways to get out of here and pick the best one.

—Okay, let's do it. Let's find three ways to get out of here.

—Okay. You go first.

—You go first.

—Are you back to repeating?

—I thought you should think of an idea first.

—My idea was you go first, and then you repeated what I said.

—Let's try to yell.

—Yell? Why not pick something we could use?

—Yelling is an idea we could use.

—We tried it before; it didn't work.

—Maybe it will work if we try again?

—Okay.

—So idea number one is yelling. Do you have a suggestion for idea number two?

—No.

—You answered too quickly.

—I answered quickly because there are no ideas.

—How about banging on the side? Maybe someone will hear us if we bang on the side.

—If they didn't hear us yell, why would they hear us bang? It doesn't make any sense.

—Number one is yelling and number two is banging on the side. Do you have any suggestions for idea number three?

—Yes.
—Yes?
—I said yes. You don't need to repeat it.
—What's your suggestion?
—We sit here. We do nothing.
—That means we'll die. You're not trying.
—There's nothing to try.
—We just ... need a plan.
—We don't have a choice.
—Of course we do.
—Don't you know what's going to happen?
—I don't want to think about it.
—In an attempt to survive we will eat our own feces and drink our own urine.
—Please.
—Next we will claw at each other's eyes and bite at each other's flesh. There will be blood. We will no longer be able to see.
—Please. Stop.
—You will be yelling and banging on the side. No one will hear. I will sit and wait. We will pass out before we take our final breaths. Our decaying bodies will fill the place with a stench that neither of us will smell.
—Will maggots form?
—I don't know. Probably.

THE ANGEL AT THE BUS STOP

A woman approached the bus stop carrying a heavy cloth bag of books. She was weary from working a job for which she was overqualified and underpaid.

It was raining, and to the woman, the raindrops looked like tears as they streamed down the windows on the buildings and cars. However, she knew this was cliché because she had a degree in literature and remembered a lesson on dead metaphors. "Her eyes were like diamonds" was an example her professor had used. The professor was young and cheerful and still hopeful about the way things might turn out. The woman, who was barely twenty at the time, thought one day she might like to be just like her teacher, and she often wondered what happened to that young professor.

Out of the corner of her eye, the woman saw what she concluded was either a ghost or an angel wearing a yellow rubber raincoat. This was not a cliché but, in fact, something she was seeing before her very eyes. The woman wanted to say something but wasn't entirely sure what. Perhaps the ghost or angel didn't want to be bothered. Perhaps he didn't want his picture taken.

But the woman thought to herself, you only live once, and leaned forward toward the ghost or angel. —Excuse me, she said, are you an angel or a ghost?

—I'm an angel, he said, fiddling with a button on his rubber coat.

—I'm excited to meet you, she said. It must be so great to be you.

She couldn't help herself. This was such a treat, the type of story she could tell her coworkers when she couldn't think of anything else to say.

—Thank you, the angel said, but I'm afraid you've bought into a myth about angels. It's not great to be me. Not even close.

—But don't you come from heaven?

—Yes, I do, the angel said.

—But to be an angel, she said, you must have done something remarkable.

—Nope, he said. Everyone gets to be an angel nowadays. It's a form of ribbon-giving, so no one feels left out.

—Surely, there must be some perks, she said.

—That's the misconception, the angel said. The working conditions for angels are terrible. Our boss is ruthless. We think he has a personality disorder but it is difficult to diagnose and treat.

The woman could not believe what she was hearing. —What about the benefits? she asked.

—There are no benefits. Last year they even got rid of the pension, so none of us can ever retire.

She gasped and put her hand to her chest. —I'm so sorry. I had no idea. I thought there would be something to look forward to.

—There's nothing to look forward to. There's not even any hope.

—But some in heaven must have it better than the rest. There must be some kind of carrot to make the angels believe that if they work hard enough, they might have a chance at a half-decent life.

The angel shook his head sadly. —It's eternity, so no one need bother pretend.

—I was going to say I wish I was you, but now I don't feel that way anymore.

—You know who has it worse off than either you or me? the angel asked. The little children who make all the clothes you wear to work. They have it worse off than anybody, if it makes you feel better.

They looked down the street. There was no sign of the bus. A silence had fallen between them. The sound of cars driving through puddles was the only sound, and it made the silence all the more unbearable.

The angel moved closer to the woman and asked —Can you spare a dollar for a cup of coffee?

—No, she said quickly. I can't spare a dollar. Besides you'll probably just spend it on alcohol and drugs.

—That's exactly what I plan to do, he said.

—I know, she said, I saw it coming.

WORLD 1

World, I'm worried about you. Everything is so sad. I had a dream I died and being dead was like being behind a glass wall where you could see and hear everything but no one could see or hear you like a fly in a jar. When you're a ghost you are constantly spying, constantly eavesdropping, but you don't have anyone to tell your secrets to—even if you witness a murder or an elaborate plot by the government against the people. When you are dead there is no CIA. Ghosts can't gossip with other ghosts. It's not part of the plan.

SPIRITS

*

At the seance of a close friend I got drunk and embarrassed myself. The spirits were annoyed because they felt I took away all the attention. Spirits often aren't good-looking and don't have much of a sense of humour.

*

Spirits have all kinds of afflictions. You wouldn't know it at first, but it's far from a peaceful way to exist.

*

I'm attending a spirit social next week. They don't like you to call it a seance anymore because of the negative connotations.

*

The first spirit I contacted was named Joe and he had OCD. He was so busy flicking the lights on and off that I couldn't get him to focus on anything else.

—Joe, do you really have OCD? I asked. Or are you just acting out?

I'm not very empathetic. I even have problems throwing out garbage and leaving the house. Sometimes your mind just can't control what your body is going to do. I knew this but couldn't help myself from being annoyed.

To irritate him, I kept asking—What does dead feel like?—over and over.

*

Does Joe believe God? He's not sure yet because he hasn't seen any god around, if that's what you're asking, but he's not ruling out the possibility. Anyway what does he know? He's only been dead a couple hundred years.

POETRY—YOU'RE POPULAR, OKAY

Poetry—you're popular, okay. I don't know why you care so much about what other people think or do. Why do you need everyone looking at you? Why do you need everyone to be your friend? Don't get your nose so out of joint all the time. You know, you don't need to put people down to feel better about yourself. One day you might have a street named after you. But probably you won't. Take a break. Take some time off once in a while and go all the way around to the back of the school to the pit where the kids go when they skip class and where they like to get stoned.

A BIRD

—A bird is trying to be my friend.

—Lucky you.

—No, he's using me. He thinks he can get something by sucking up.

—What can he get?

—Chips or part of my hot dog.

—Can't you share? Can't you give him some?

—I'm not interested in beggars or handouts.

—But he needs to eat and has no money. He has no way to earn a living and he's drowning in all that debt.

—That has nothing to do with me. I have chips and a hot dog because my parents scrimped and saved so that I would have a future. Don't make me feel guilty that there's nothing left for that bird.

—That kind of makes you a beggar too. You got something for nothing.

—Nope, it just makes me lucky.

THE HYPOCHONDRIAC

The hypochondriac was in a constant state of paradox because she also had a secret death wish. But she really was sick of focussing on herself so she decided to turn her fear of disease and suffering on everyone around her instead. She started telling family, friends, strangers their moles had cancer, they were developing Parkinson's, their babies might be stillborn, their hair was falling out and they would soon be bald. She told them their cellphones were giving them brain tumours, they were suffering from bone density loss, a stroke was imminent, they had blood clots in their lungs. She diagnosed cysts, scabies, lice, eye sores, and venereal diseases. But it was shingles that was, surprisingly, the biggest hit at parties.

ROUGHING IT IN THE BUSH

With my being allowed to eat the servants, I felt sorry I had in my possession a curious Japanese sword—broad, three-sided in the blade, and in shape, a moving snake; this circumstance gave the weapon great value. For several days, they continued to visit the house, bringing along with them some fresh companion.

BUS RIDE

I was on a bus. Then the bus stopped. The driver yelled something to the passengers that I couldn't understand and everyone was getting up to leave.

So I got off too. I was alone in the middle of an empty suburb. All the houses looked the same. Small and sad-looking with dirty white aluminum siding.

War houses. In all the houses, the windows were dark and the blinds closed. It didn't look like anyone was watching TV.

It was winter. I was wearing a winter coat, but I didn't have gloves or a scarf. Mounds of snow were piled on the front lawns. Melting ice formed puddles on the sidewalks. Sometimes there was ice under the puddles that made someone walking on the sidewalk slip.

Thankfully, I was wearing a backpack that helped break my fall and prevented injuries to the back of my head.

I opened the backpack and discovered there was no wallet inside. There was a pencil case and a black binder. I opened the binder and found notes. The notes were written in English but did not form words I could comprehend. They did not indicate where I was going or where I had been.

I put the binder in the backpack and walked down the street where the bus had dropped me off. Everything was quiet, and I could see my breath.

A car drove by. The person was wearing a ski mask. I waved as he drove by, and he ignored me. Up ahead was a group of teenagers. They were laughing and pushing each other into the dirty snow banks. I looked at the ground as I walked past. The teenagers ignored me.

Further up the street, I saw a strip mall. As I got closer, I discovered that all the stores were closed except a small variety store on the far end. I went inside. The clerk wore braces.

I said hello and asked if he had a pay phone. The clerk shook his head and said no, but that I could use the phone from the store as long as it wasn't long distance.

"It's not," I said and picked up the phone. Then I realized I had no one to call and put the phone back on its cradle. "Thanks anyway," I said.

Just as I was leaving, the man with the ski mask walked into the store and demanded all the money from the till. The clerk handed him the money because the man with the ski mask had a gun.

The gun was pointed at me, and the man with the ski mask told me to empty my backpack. I emptied the pencil case and the binder onto the floor.

The man with the ski mask said, "I've been looking for this." He grabbed the binder and left.

"Why did you give that to him?" the clerk asked.

"Why did you give him the money?" I asked.

"I didn't give him any money."

"I saw you give him money from the till."

"I think you better leave. The police will be here any minute, and they'll arrest you."

Outside, the teenagers were still throwing each other into snow banks. The man with the ski mask was gone and so was his car.

I continued to walk down the road where the bus stopped. I was thinking about a scarf and then I was thinking about gloves. I was thinking about the bus and where it went and why it didn't come back.

I saw a sign. At first I thought it was a stop sign and then a yield sign and then a speed bump sign. As I approached it, I discovered it was a bus stop sign. I stood under it, hoping a bus would come and I could get on.

It was getting darker. A person walked toward me. He was wearing a ski mask and carrying a black binder.

"Do you know what time the bus comes?" he asked.

"No," I said.

"Could you do me a favour?" he asked. "If I pass out before the bus comes, will you resuscitate me? With artificial respiration?"

"I don't think I could do that," I said. "I'm not trained."

"Of course you are trained. I took the course with you." He opened the black binder and showed me the notes he had taken on artificial respiration. "What did you get on the last test? I got an A."

"I got an A too," I said.

"Don't you think the professor is a pervert the way he grabs women's tits?"

"I haven't seen him do that," I said.

"The tits on the dummies."

"I haven't seen him do that either."

"Would you like a ride home?" he said. "I live just up the road, and I have my car there."

"Do you still have that gun?"

"I don't own a gun."

"You had a gun in the store when you took my binder."

"If you want to photocopy my notes, go ahead. I don't mind sharing."

We walked on the road, where it was dry. The man with the ski mask kept saying his house was a few blocks away every few blocks.

We cut through two backyards. The man with the ski mask said not to worry, he knew all the neighbours, and they liked him. I followed him through a wooded area and across a ravine. When we finally got to his house, he told me to wait on the front porch while he talked to his wife.

"Are you sure it's no trouble? I'll find another way home."

“Of course it’s no trouble. It’s no trouble for family.”

The man with the ski mask went inside. I could hear voices. I heard a child talking and then laughing and then crying.

The man with the ski mask came out onto the porch and lit a cigarette.

“She just has to get the kids ready. We’re going out anyway. We’re going to the train station too.”

The man’s wife came outside with four little girls. They filed off the porch and got into the car.

“This is my professor.”

“Are you going to give him an A?”

“I already did,” I said.

“That’s good,” she said. “It sounds like a hard course, but what do I know? I was never any good at school anyway.”

WORLD 2

World, I can't stand you. I'm trying to be as literal as possible so you can understand what I'm trying to say. When you continue to bring in more people, you are contributing to the problem. I'm a hypocrite. All I like to do is complain, but I rarely do anything else. I pretend my rage is directed at everyone but really it's myself I hate. I never asked to be born. Neither did he, but he made the best of it. All I do is cry about what is not fair. So, so what? I better go. The espresso maker is on fire again.

THE BLOB

—A blob is sitting on the couch because people have become blobs. People can also time travel and talk to each other from the future and the past.

—You mean when you are fifty you can talk to your husband when he was ten and he'll talk back to you?

—Yes. Or your mother or sister or your best friend.

—That is confusing.

—It's how we communicate now. We've solved the issue of time.

—It sounds like we've made time more confusing.

—You're just saying that because you are ten. When you are seventy like me, you will understand how great it is. You'll understand that you as a seventy-year-old have been worn down by life and lost all of your pizazz. For example, I'd rather talk to my husband before he had all those back problems. I'd rather talk to that version of him than the person he is now. Now he's always sore, always complaining. Nothing is good enough.

—It sounds like you are putting him down. It sounds like you don't like him anymore.

—Not at all. In fact, since the time travel, we hardly ever fight.

—Can you do more than talk? Can you play Scrabble?

—No, everyone's a blob.

—What do you do then?

—We just sit on the couch and stare and talk to various versions of ourselves from the past.

—What's the point of that?

PARDON ME

for Gary Barwin

"Pardon me," I said. "I thought you were a hillbilly dancing to Aretha Franklin with a fat raccoon."

"I'm not," he said. "But haven't I heard that line before?"

"You have. It's from a Richard Brautigan book—only the narrator mistakes a woman for a trout stream, and I'm mistaking you for something else."

"Brautigan's line is better."

"Yes, it is. Because it's timeless. You can mistake a woman for a trout stream at any point in history," I said.

"The English teacher would call that plagiarism," he said.

"She would, but the English teacher is not a credible source because she wants to kill herself."

"Is she fat like the raccoon?" he asked.

"Yes, that fat," I said.

NO LEGS OR ARMS

My husband and I were at the ranch house of an acquaintance of my husband's cousin. White wall-to-wall carpeting sprawled from room to room. The décor was minimal—white leather couches, brass tables fitted with glass tops. The hostess, a long-legged brunette, served tuna and egg salad sandwiches with the crusts cut off. We heard kids somewhere else in the house. The hostess turned up the stereo and classical music played.

For a while I stood there awkwardly with my husband, his stepmother, his cousins, and the hostess. Then a fifteen-year-old girl came out of her room and poured a glass of milk. The girl had the same legs as the mother—long and thin. She was wearing sandals and her toes were painted red. The girl looked over at me and said hi. I smiled but didn't feel like talking to her, so I picked up a tuna sandwich and walked out of the kitchen with everyone else and into the living room where the hostess was about to start a parlour game.

As the hostess explained the complicated rules, a crash came from the kitchen. It was the hostess's daughter splayed out on the kitchen floor. One leg was behind her head and the other was cracked in two. I approached the girl and tried to help her up. No, please don't, she said. I have a toothache. I'm sorry to hear that, I said. I felt bad for leaving her in the kitchen all alone. Then she said, You see my legs? They're not real. They're prosthetics. I leaned in and took a closer look at the legs. They looked like the wooden legs on a mannequin. I just wore fake legs so I could be normal, she cried, and so everyone would stop making fun of me because I have a toothache.

Just then my husband's stepmother came into the room, and I took a closer look at her legs. They were wooden too. Are you looking at my legs? my husband's stepmother said. I nodded. They're not real, she said, and neither are my arms. She and I, his stepmother pointed to the girl, went to the same surgeon. You mean all this time, you've had no legs or arms? No legs or arms, she repeated. I turned to my husband, Did you know about this? No, he said. I'm just as shocked as you. What if we took them off? I asked. Then I would just have a body.

Why didn't you tell us? I asked. Because, she pointed to the girl on the floor, like her, I wanted to be normal. I wanted to be like everyone else. Is it like wearing makeup to cover a scar? I asked. Yes, she said, it's exactly like that.

WORLD 3

What is the world going to do with so many good parents? Everyone will be so well-adjusted. There's not going to be enough jobs for all the people who can and will do good work.

THE SEANCE

—The spirits at my seance are not allowed to talk about the 1960s or how cellphones have changed the way we communicate. In fact, there should be no discussion of technology at all. The colour scheme for my séance will be yellow and red.

—Are you at all worried people won't come to your séance and that in the end no one really cares?

—Even murderers are interested in spirits. Even murderers will take the time to talk to the dead. Sometimes they'll leave a tip or a little note with their phone number on it.

—Do spirits get worked up if they don't like the menu or don't feel up to having something to eat?

—Spirits are always courteous to the waitress. They almost never slap her ass or attack her on her way to the car from the parking garage.

—Do spirits mind telling you how much money they make in a year or how often they get paid?

—Sometimes spirits are snobs, but don't let that discourage you.

HE SAID

He said.
She said.
She said.
She said.
She said.
She said.
She said.
She said.
She said.
She said.

HARPER

1.

His belly is full from eating too much rich food against his mother's advice. But that's the problem with him—he won't listen to anyone, and now he has a tummy ache. But we can't blame him because he's just a babe, a toddler grabbing with chubby small hands at all the things he sees and wants for himself, crying to anyone who is interested enough to listen—mine, mine, mine.

2.

When his mother knit scarves, he liked to hide behind the couch and giggle. And when the scarf was long enough and part of it dragged on the floor and went a little ways under the couch, so he could just reach it with his tiny pink hand, he would tug at the end of the scarf she had put so much time into—the scarf that would have one day been his. He was most clever at pulling the wool so gently she could not feel the unravelling of all she had done.

3.

At the birthday party, he was the only one who didn't bring a present. He didn't even say happy birthday to his host because, well, that was just who he was. Wasn't it enough that he was there? Wasn't it enough he took the time to show up?

4.

He's unteachable, his fourth-grade teacher said to his mother and father on parent-teacher night. His mother thought the school smelled like sweat and the flickering fluorescent lights bothered his father's sensitive eyes. His teacher, Mrs. Brown, was that one teacher that all the children adored. He doesn't believe in anything I try to teach him. He thinks he can answer however he wants on a quiz, and if he's told his answers are wrong, he just tears up his sheet into tiny pieces and scatters them on the floor. I've never seen anything like it, she said. Where did he get such an attitude? What will become of him?

5.

His nickname in high school was sugar tits, and every day he would run home to his mother's arms and weep tears the size of gumdrops. He wanted so badly to fit in. But when his father bought the variety store, the one on the corner closest to the school, and he let all the popular kids eat as much candy as they wanted for free, he suddenly had friends. It wasn't for his personality that they liked him but for what he was willing to sacrifice for their pleasure—his own father. Although his mother was happy her son had formed new friendships, she missed the time they spent together after school. She missed holding her son—who was almost, but not quite yet a grown man—like a baby in her arms.

MEXICO

I was talking to my friend on the phone and told her about a dream I had where I was in Mexico walking past houses that had no front walls and how I could see all the people living in their houses, eating and sleeping and cleaning, like a doll's house.

—That happened to me when I was in Mexico, my friend said.

—No, it was just a dream I had.

—I was just telling someone else the exact same story about all the people in the houses with no walls that everyone could see into, she said.

Then I was struck with a thought. What if I dream other people's memories from now on or what if all of our dreams are really just other people's memories—a kind of collective unconscious?

—I think I figured out the meaning of life, I shouted into the phone so loud it woke up her sleeping baby who started to cry.

What are you going to do now that you've figured out the meaning of life?

—I think I should tell someone, I said.

—If I were you, I wouldn't tell anybody, she said. They might lock you up.

—That wouldn't be so bad, I said.

—Of course it would. It would be horrible.

—Do you know what would be horrible? Being buried alive.

—I've always been more afraid of going to the mental institution than being buried alive, she said. I used to have dreams of men in white coats coming into the basement to take me away.

—So who should I tell? I asked.

—About what?

—About the meaning of life.

—Oh that, she said. I don't know. I wasn't paying attention.

SKYLER

she's totally gross when trying to be sexy she's still a bitch she's just protecting her own interests the only thing I am sure of Skyler looks out for Skyler I wanted her dead but if she does stay on his side then she may live FINALLY dumb bitch I punched my TV screen when she said I fucked him I'd bash her if I saw her in life why the fuck did she go meet him she should have spoken to her husband first then go meet him so FUCKING STUPID she's money hungry you will meet people in life with punchable faces Skyler is one of them bitch doesn't understand dinner small talk I really really want him to just smack her over the face with his metal crutches and end the bitch someone should shoot her that's all I have to say I'd totally fuck her I will wack this bitch I would never lay my hands on a women but I would dead set fuck her up with a chain saw not a team player goddamn I hate this vindictive bitch hoer I'm waiting for him to kill her I want to fuck her face with a cactus fuck this bitch whore slut she's a piece of shit we need to somehow trick this bitch onto a rocket and shoot it into the fucking sun or a black hole either one is fine fucking hate this bitch shittest wife and mother award goes to Skyler fuck her fat sea cow head such a fat fucking head WHY IS SHE SUCH A CUNT finally I'll be honest bitch is such a buzz kill Skyler needs to die she was cool then she fucked him who is she I just want to ask who the fuck is Skyler wish he would round-house kick her to the jaw such a fucking bitch FUCK YOU SKYLER FUCK YOU dam hoe kill her dumbass Skyler is the biggest bitch ever fucking hate that slut I fucking hate you bitch quality somebody slap this broad there is hope for humanity after all fuck Skyler in the nostril with a red hot poker normally people look a lot nicer when they smile but when she does I get scared rotten fag hag I have this theory that if you cut off all her hair she'd look like a British man sometimes I dream about killing Skyler those dreams end wet and sticky she's gotta go this bitch shit cunt words cannot describe how much of a fucking mole she is I'll kill this bitch with fire she's a dumb hoe bag fucking hate this bitch she does me in hard what a filthy fukn slut royal pain in the ass hope she dies badly oh my god yes btch needs to shut the fuck up and suck his dick just do it you dirtyyyyy little whoreee hahaaaaa I friggin' can't stand her filthy slut I woulda backhanded the bitch fuckin' ruins everything such a crazy bitch I hope she get's cancer and dies get off the dick and on the pip bitch you need to shut your mouth and cook your son some mother fuckin' breakfast I hate this fucking slut I hate this gonad crushing slut it sure seems like she's finally standing by her man

WORLD 4

How old were you when you realized the world was a nightmare from which you could never wake?

I ALWAYS WANT TO BE ALONE,
I HATE EVERYONE

I am not a busybody.
I don't care what the neighbours are doing.

I hate people because I don't trust them.
Too many come across as fake.

People want me to be like them, and it's never going to happen.
I need quality people.

I am going to come across mean.
This is one of my survivor skills.

I have bad days but I'm actually improving.
Everyone should try and get out in this world.

I think people aren't going to like me,
so I make sure I never meet them in the first place.

Everyone else is on earth.
I am the one so far from earth—no one can touch me.

This is lonely, isn't it?
Please forgive me if I have harmed you in any way.

I hate people who refuse to eat vegetables.
Do you by chance have an IUD? I experienced similar issues with mine.

It's a little pricey but if it helps me, I'm willing to pay it.

A CONSPIRACY TO HARM

Texter, Questioner, Ruler, Crier, and Crowd are enjoying a sunny day in the park where children play and a stream burbles nearby. Pisser is standing by the edge of the water with his back to everyone else.

Texter is on his phone sending a text message when Questioner approaches.

QUESTIONER: Hey, man, what's going on?

TEXTER: *(looks up briefly)* Not much.

QUESTIONER: *(points to Pisser)* What's that guy doing over there by the stream?

TEXTER: *(glances at Pisser then back down at his phone)* Oh, him? He's pissing in the water supply.

QUESTIONER: Won't it make them sick?

TEXTER: Yes, it will make everyone sick. We will soon have no water to drink or use to bathe or wash our clothes or our dinner dishes or our newly paved streets.

QUESTIONER: Why doesn't anyone stop him? Look at all these people around.

TEXTER: Because he's making a lot of money and Ruler decided Pisser can do whatever he wants. Pisser wouldn't be so bad if he had a small bladder. But the problem is that his bladder is big. There's no end to all the piss.

QUESTIONER: Has anyone tried to stop him?

TEXTER: Oh, yes, Crier has tried to stop him, but no one will listen. No one thinks they have the time.

QUESTIONER: Aren't they worried about their water?

TEXTER: They think their water comes in a bottle and the bottle will always be on the shelf. They think Ruler will take care of them and their families. He tells them this and they believe him. But really he's just worried about making money so he can buy his way into heaven.

QUESTIONER: What about you? What are you doing?

TEXTER: I'm sending a text message to my friends at work. We're going to the bar to drink and complain about how little money we make and how much we hate our boss. Then I'm going to get drunker than anyone else and throw up in the parking lot. When I finally get home, I'm going to eat a grilled cheese sandwich with ketchup and pickles and then cry myself to sleep. In the morning, I'll wake up late and have to skip my shower. Then I'll go into work with a bad hangover and have to drink a lot of water to get rid of it.

QUESTIONER: And the piss?

TEXTER: Oh, yes, the piss. Eventually, sooner rather than later, I'll have to drink that too.

I WISH I THOUGHT OF EVERYTHING FIRST

I'm crying into my thunderstorm.

I don't think we have the same taste in apocalypses.

You smell like TV.

Your government is a selfie.

We would all be better off if we just worried about how good we look in our phones.

I make no pronouncements.

I'm feeling the rage again.

It's a stupid form.

From one prison to the next.

I like your projection.

Most things aren't worth fighting for.

Everything is cute. Nothing is a waste of time.

Your poems are killing me.

Stop trying to make me a pervert.

I think my rage is coming across as rage.

I wish I thought of everything first.

He accuses her of baby talk.

The object you liked has been removed by its owner and can no longer be liked.

I'm pretty sure everybody deserves to be hated.

Why are they trying to scare us so much?

We are all complicit in the system. Just in case you think none of this is your fault.

I did my best.

Everyone fucks good even stupid people.

WORLD 5

World, if I were you, I would give up. Stop trying so hard. Stop trying to be something you're not. You're so big, you're busting. You're about to explode and everyone here is tired of listening to you talk about yourself. We just want to hear someone else's voice for a change. We just want to go home.

YOUR POEM SHOULD HAVE FOUR LEGS

Your poem should have four legs.
Your poem should wear a hat in the sun.
Your poem should get plastic surgery or a non-invasive chemical peel.
If your poem is getting too old, lie about its age.
Your poem should be more like his poem.
Your poem needs to lighten up a little.
Your poem needs to take anti-depressants.
Your poem should see a dentist.
Your poem should mock all other poems.
Your poem needs a boob job.
Your poem needs to get a sense of humour.
Your poem should stop drinking.
Your poem should stop getting offended.
Your poem should lock itself up and throw away the key.
Your poem needs vaginal rejuvenation surgery—just for itself, not for anyone else.
Your poem should have a good author photo.
Your poem needs more lipstick.
Your poem should embarrass itself.
Your poem should hurt everyone else's feelings.
Your poem should try acid.
Your poem should get its tubes tied.
Your poem should be sent away to camp for the entire summer.
Your poem should learn to knit in a café.
Your poem should be like everyone else's poem.
Your poem should finger itself.
Your poem should finger everyone else.
Your poem should go get fucked.
Your poem needs to get a day job.
Your poem should be on a floor hockey team.
Your poem needs a feeding tube.

Your poem should take the Rorschach test.
Your poem needs seventeen more followers.
Your poem should find a hobby.
Your poem should blog.
Your poem should sing folk songs on the weekends.
When undressing, your poem should use the private
change room.
Your poem shouldn't let its genitals show.
Your poem should like to be roughed up a bit.
Your poem should spot clean.
Your poem needs to be more like a selfie.
Your poem should get its period.
Your poem should learn pain management.
Your poem should look pretty and shut up.
Your poem should have a boner.
Your poem should smell like a wax museum or jail.
Your poem should not walk alone at night.
Your poem should drink itself to death.
Your poem should be born between 1946 and 1964.
Your poem should be enjoying its sabbatical.
Your poem should first appear fun-loving and then be nasty.
Your poem should start in a waiting room and end in a car.
Your poem should watch its waistline.
Your poem should murder everyone or no one.
Your poem should be in love with itself.
Your poem should get a room.
Your poem should have access to contraceptives.
Your poem should stop sucking its thumb.
Your poem should go to a movie sometime or read a book.
Your poem should look good on a coffee table.
Your poem should annoy all other poems.
Your poem should have an attaché case.
Your poem should squirt.

Your poem should complain about the weather.
Your poem should pretend to say nothing.
Your poem should be literal.
Your poem should be understood by everyone or no one.
Your poem should have low self-esteem.
Your poem should feign humility.
Your poem should take the stairs.
Your poem should hide its obsessive-compulsive disorder.
Your poem should package itself for a grant.
Your poem should live in the future.
Your poem should assume no one is looking.
Your poem should assume no one cares.
Your poem should be a wet dream.
Your poem should be sticky and smell like cheese.
Your poem should not step in the vomit.
Your poem should be reclusive.
Your poem needs to make a lot of friends.
Your poem should never admit it's a poem.
Your poem should stop an awkward conversation.
Your poem should stop saying things it doesn't mean.

WORLD 6

World, I'm weak these days. I'm tired. I barely have the energy to pick up a pen. I wish— I can't even tell you what I wish for anymore because I forgot where I left it. Probably in some drawer in the back of my closet where it sits collecting dust, collecting mould.

APRIL 30 – MAY 31, 2014

A WOMAN WAS SEXUALLY ASSAULTED IN WILLENHALL AFTER SHE WAS FOLLOWED HOME FOLLOWING A NIGHT OUT.

POLICE ARE MAKING ENQUIRIES AND APPEALING FOR WITNESSES AFTER A WOMAN WAS SEXUALLY ASSAULTED LAST NIGHT.

A MAN HAS BEEN ARRESTED AFTER A WOMAN WAS SEXUALLY ASSAULTED IN THE MCCOWAN ROAD AND MCNICOLL AVENUE AREA THURSDAY, MAY 29.

A WOMAN WAS SEXUALLY ASSAULTED AND ATTACKED BY A GANG OF MEN IN A WEST CORNWALL TOWN, POLICE SAY.

DETECTIVES ARE APPEALING FOR WITNESSES AFTER A WOMAN WAS SEXUALLY ASSAULTED AS SHE WAS WALKING HOME IN GLOSSOP.

RICHLAND COUNTY DEPUTIES ARE INVESTIGATING AFTER A WOMAN WAS SEXUALLY ASSAULTED WHILE WALKING HER DOG.

A WOMAN WAS SEXUALLY ASSAULTED BY TWO MEN TUESDAY NIGHT IN A FIELD OFF VERSAILLES ROAD, LEXINGTON POLICE SAID.

POLICE ARE APPEALING FOR WITNESSES TO COME FORWARD AFTER A WOMAN WAS SEXUALLY ASSAULTED ON A TRAIN BETWEEN CENTRAL AND PENRITH EARLIER THIS MONTH.

A WOMAN WAS SEXUALLY ASSAULTED IN MELBOURNE LAST NIGHT, JUST ONE WEEK AFTER TWO OTHER WOMEN WERE ATTACKED IN THE SAME AREA.

A WOMAN WAS SEXUALLY ASSAULTED AS SHE SLEPT ON A TRAIN AFTER ENJOYING A NIGHT OUT WITH FRIENDS IN LONDON.

POLICE ARE LOOKING FOR A SUSPECT AFTER A WOMAN WAS SEXUALLY ASSAULTED IN DOWNTOWN REGINA OVER THE WEEKEND.

POLICE IN CORBY ARE APPEALING FOR WITNESSES AFTER A WOMAN WAS SEXUALLY ASSAULTED IN THE TOWN.

VANCOUVER POLICE ARE INVESTIGATING AFTER A WOMAN WAS SEXUALLY ASSAULTED JOGGING THROUGH STANLEY PARK MONDAY MORNING.

SOUTH WALES POLICE ARE INVESTIGATING ALLEGATIONS A WOMAN WAS SEXUALLY ASSAULTED IN A VW VAN IN JERSEY MARINE.

ACCORDING TO POLICE, ON THURSDAY, MAY 1, AROUND 10:30 P.M., A WOMAN WAS SEXUALLY ASSAULTED ON COMO LAKE AVENUE NEAR WESTWOOD STREET.

HYDERABAD: DESPITE CLAIMS OF THE CYBERABAD POLICE OF INTENSE PATROLLING ON THE OUTER RING ROAD (ORR), A WOMAN WAS SEXUALLY ASSAULTED, STABBED AND LEFT TO DIE ON THE EIGHT-LANE CARRIAGEWAY AT HIMAYATSAGAR LATE ON WEDNESDAY NIGHT.

A WOMAN WAS SEXUALLY ASSAULTED NEAR WASTE GROUND IN CORBY WHERE A DOG WALKER WAS STABBED JUST DAYS EARLIER.

POLICE APPEAL FOR WITNESSES AFTER A WOMAN WAS SEXUALLY ASSAULTED ON A TRAIN BETWEEN CENTRAL AND PENRITH.

THE SEARCH IS ON FOR A SUSPECT, AFTER POLICE SAY A WOMAN WAS SEXUALLY ASSAULTED IN STORM LAKE, IOWA.

A WOMAN WAS SEXUALLY ASSAULTED IN BRUNSWICK ON FRIDAY NIGHT, A WEEK AFTER TWO WOMEN WERE ATTACKED IN THE SAME AREA AFTER LEAVING SYDNEY ROAD BARS.

POLICE ARE APPEALING FOR INFORMATION AFTER A WOMAN WAS SEXUALLY ASSAULTED WHILST TRAVELLING ON A BUS TO HYDE.

TORONTO POLICE ARE ASKING THE PUBLIC FOR HELP IDENTIFYING TWO SUSPECTS AFTER A WOMAN WAS SEXUALLY ASSAULTED AND HELD AGAINST HER WILL FOR 28 HOURS LAST WEEKEND.

A WOMAN WAS SEXUALLY ASSAULTED WHILE WALKING ON A STREET IN CENTRAL QUEENSLAND AT THE WEEKEND.

DURHAM—POLICE SAY A WOMAN WAS SEXUALLY ASSAULTED BY A MAN WITH A KNIFE LAST WEEKEND, AND THEY ARE ASKING THE PUBLIC'S HELP IN FINDING A SUSPECT THE WOMAN DESCRIBED.

COQUITLAM MOUNTIES ARE HUNTING FOR A SUSPECT AFTER A WOMAN WAS SEXUALLY ASSAULTED MAY 1ST.

A WOMAN WAS SEXUALLY ASSAULTED IN EDINBURGH LATE LAST NIGHT.

A WOMAN WAS SEXUALLY ASSAULTED AS SHE WALKED IN STRETFORD.

WOMAN DRAGGED, SEXUALLY ASSAULTED NEAR HUMBOLDT PARK.

POLICE HAVE ISSUED A FRESH APPEAL FOR WITNESSES AFTER A WOMAN WAS SEXUALLY ASSAULTED IN HER HOME BY AN INTRUDER LAST WEEK.

POLICE SAY THAT A WOMAN WAS SEXUALLY ASSAULTED EARLY YESTERDAY IN BED-STUY.

RESIDENTS IN SOUTH SUBURBAN MATTESON ARE ON ALERT AFTER A WOMAN WAS SEXUALLY ASSAULTED NEAR A METRA TRAIN STATION.

A WOMAN WAS SEXUALLY ASSAULTED THIS MORNING ON ST. ANDREWS ROAD AS SHE WALKED HOME FROM A NIGHT OUT.

HAMILTON POLICE ARE LOOKING FOR A MALE SUSPECT AFTER A WOMAN WAS SEXUALLY ASSAULTED WHILE LEAVING THE HAMILTON-BRANTFORD RAIL TRAIL.

POLICE HAVE LAUNCHED AN INVESTIGATION AFTER A WOMAN WAS SEXUALLY ASSAULTED IN GLASGOW'S KELVINGROVE PARK.

POLICE ARE APPEALING FOR WITNESSES TO COME FORWARD AFTER A WOMAN WAS SEXUALLY ASSAULTED IN WILLENHALL OVER THE WEEKEND.

POLICE ARE APPEALING FOR WITNESSES AFTER A WOMAN WAS SEXUALLY ASSAULTED IN THE EARLY HOURS OF THE MORNING IN CHESTERFIELD.

A WOMAN WAS SEXUALLY ASSAULTED AND ROBBED NEAR THE ALBANY COLLEGE OF PHARMACY, SAGE COLLEGE OF ALBANY, AND ALBANY LAW SCHOOL CAMPUS, ACCORDING TO A LETTER SENT TO STUDENTS FROM THE UNIVERSITY HEIGHTS ASSOCIATION PUBLIC SAFETY.

A YOUNG MAN IS BEING SOUGHT BY POLICE AFTER A WOMAN WAS SEXUALLY ASSAULTED IN PALMERSTON NORTH AT THE WEEKEND.

A WOMAN WAS SEXUALLY ASSAULTED AT ABOUT 4:30 A.M. IN ROOM 1 ON THE GROUND FLOOR OF VISINTAINER'S MOTEL EARLY TUESDAY MORNING.

POLICE ARE ISSUING AN E-FIT LIKENESS OF AN OFFENDER, AFTER A WOMAN WAS SEXUALLY ASSAULTED IN IPSWICH AS SHE WAS WALKING HOME THROUGH A PARK.

POLICE SAID A WOMAN WAS SEXUALLY ASSAULTED AT 4 A.M. IN THE 100 BLOCK OF OAKLEIGH AVENUE.

POLICE ARE URGING ANYONE WITH INFORMATION TO COME FORWARD AFTER A WOMAN WAS SEXUALLY ASSAULTED ON A BUS FROM ERDINGTON.

A WOMAN WAS SEXUALLY ASSAULTED IN WALKABOUT #BRISTOL IN EARLY HRS OF LAST SUNDAY — IF YOU KNOW THIS MAN PLS CALL 101.

A WOMAN WAS SEXUALLY ASSAULTED WHILE USING THE PATH.

A WOMAN WAS SEXUALLY ASSAULTED AT THE RIVERWALK THURSDAY NIGHT.

POLICE TELL THE DEMOCRAT-HERALD THAT A WOMAN WAS SEXUALLY ASSAULTED BY AN ARMED MAN IN ONE OF THE BREAK-INS, AND IN ANOTHER A 6-YEAR-OLD BOY WOKE HIS MOTHER TO TELL HER SOMEONE WAS IN THE HOUSE.

A WOMAN WAS SEXUALLY ASSAULTED AROUND 10:45 P.M. MAY 17 AFTER BOARDING THE TRAIN AT WILSHIRE/ WESTERN STATION. IN ONE MONTH, STUDENTS RECEIVED FIVE E-MAILS ABOUT CASES INCLUDING ONE IN WHICH A 61-YEAR-OLD MAN GRABBED A STUDENT IN THE LIBRARY AND ONE IN WHICH A WOMAN WAS SEXUALLY ASSAULTED BY A MAN SHE DIDN'T KNOW IN A CAMPUS RESIDENCE.

A WOMAN WAS SEXUALLY ASSAULTED AND THROWN OUT OF A MOVING TRAIN NEAR MANDYA ON THE WAY TO MYSORE TWO YEARS AGO.

SACRAMENTO POLICE SAY A WOMAN WAS SEXUALLY ASSAULTED LATE SATURDAY NIGHT NEAR THE INTERSECTION OF FOLSOM BOULEVARD AND BICENTENNIAL CIRCLE.

IN JANUARY, A WOMAN WAS SEXUALLY ASSAULTED AT A DANCE PARTY WEST OF CAMPUS. THAT SAME MONTH, THREE PEEPING TOMS WERE SEEN WEST OF UCLA.

A WOMAN WAS SEXUALLY ASSAULTED IN MELBOURNE LAST NIGHT, JUST ONE WEEK AFTER TWO OTHER WOMEN WERE ATTACKED IN THE SAME AREA.

A WOMAN WAS SEXUALLY ASSAULTED WHEN AN ARMED MAN CAME INTO HER APARTMENT THROUGH A SECOND-FLOOR BALCONY DOOR.

WOMAN SEXUALLY ASSAULTED IN CAR PARK ATTACK.

AN INVESTIGATION HAS BEEN LAUNCHED AFTER A WOMAN WAS SEXUALLY ASSAULTED IN SCARBOROUGH.

DURHAM POLICE SAID A WOMAN WAS SEXUALLY ASSAULTED IN A RESIDENCE ON ROCHELLE STREET THURSDAY MORNING. POLICE INVESTIGATE AFTER A WOMAN WAS SEXUALLY ASSAULTED IN PENZANCE.

A WOMAN WAS SEXUALLY ASSAULTED AS SHE TRIED TO GET INTO HER CENTER CITY APARTMENT ON THURSDAY NIGHT, POLICE SAID.

A WOMAN WAS SEXUALLY ASSAULTED ON APRIL 29TH BETWEEN 2:15 P.M. AND 2:30 P.M., AT A HOME IN THE VICINITY OF RANCHO BUENA VISTA HIGH SCHOOL.

POLICE SAY A WOMAN WAS SEXUALLY ASSAULTED BY A STRANGER WHO PROVIDED HELP AFTER HER CAR RAN OUT OF GAS IN THE MIDDLE OF THE NIGHT.

A WOMAN WAS SEXUALLY ASSAULTED BY A "CROSS-EYED" MAN WHO FOLLOWED HER DOWN A DURHAM CITY STREET.

A WOMAN WAS SEXUALLY ASSAULTED BY A MAN.

A WOMAN WAS SEXUALLY ASSAULTED AND ROBBED WEDNESDAY MORNING NEAR AN L STOP IN THE ROGERS PARK NEIGHBORHOOD.

POLICE HAVE RELEASED IMAGES OF A MAN THEY WANT TO TRACE AFTER A WOMAN WAS SEXUALLY ASSAULTED ON A BUS IN BIRMINGHAM.

POLICE ARE APPEALING FOR WITNESSES AFTER A WOMAN WAS SEXUALLY ASSAULTED IN WIGAN.

A 22-YEAR-OLD TORONTO MAN IS FACING MULTIPLE CHARGES AFTER POLICE SAY A WOMAN WAS SEXUALLY ASSAULTED AFTER ANSWERING HER APARTMENT DOOR.

THIRD WOMAN ATTACKED. A WOMAN WAS SEXUALLY ASSAULTED IN BRUNSWICK ON FRIDAY NIGHT.

A TEENAGER HAS BEEN ARRESTED AFTER A WOMAN WAS SEXUALLY ASSAULTED IN SOUTH LANARKSHIRE AT THE WEEKEND.

A WOMAN WAS SEXUALLY ASSAULTED SUNDAY MORNING AFTER A GUNMAN FORCED HIS WAY INTO HER SUV IN BROKEN ARROW, AUTHORITIES SAID.

WORLD 7

World, please stop. I can't take it anymore. Every day seems worse than the last. When is it time for you to retire? You've done well for yourself. I'm sure you've racked up a pretty pension. If you don't like your job anymore, just quit. Why do you have to drag us down with you? You haven't been right for some time now. Just go. It's not like we can't get along without you. No one is essential. Everyone can and will be replaced.

YOU LOOK LIKE A PUPPET

*

I had a cap pistol.
You're a dead German.
Life is intermittent matter;
let's talk about it.

*

I think he winked at me;
that's what empathy is.

*

Let me be Roy.
You can't because you're a girl.
I'm a mutt. I belong to nothing.

*

Liberated, spoiled selfish.
Eye on the ball.
I'm very good with death.

*

I'm fluid, but
you look like an embryo.

*

We've pissed where we eat.
Of course it's art.
Am I getting too heavy?

*

This disease has been eating my sinuses.
It's fascinating.
Yes, it's disgusting.
Right.

*

You're watching your busy head.
I see a butterfly, I go for a swim.
Have you never been sad?

*

I'm not a feminist.
In a way it's a lie to get you to see the truth.

*

I'm born the week of death.
Why did I do that?
It was a way to get money to smoke.

*

Everything I am I'm not.
I'm sad.
I'm not a herd animal.
I don't want to be a robin.
You'd never know.
I guess it's not Christian.

*

I want to talk to you about God.
I'm no good at mornings. I'll go out and visit him.
He's a character.
How many times have I been told that?

*

I never liked poetry.
Not at all.
All that pettiness.

*

They were converted into consumers.
They just didn't have another plan.
What have you got?
Light drugs. A corrupt lawyer.
Some of them are nice.
So they say.

*

Birds that came to me to die
were so envious and competitive,
and surprisingly unorthodox.

*

It's theatrical
because of the illness.
You think?
Basically
our nerves are worn thin.
Sometimes I wish I could have that character.
It's a jumpy head.
Well, what would you say?
You're stealing from it.

*

What are you rebelling against?
The home contained unhappy women.
Why are you whining?
The wives were unhappy.
You're being hammered with negativity.
You look like a puppet.

*

I was a criminal.
I was a
love bandit.
You can be the German.

THE HOSPITAL

At the hospital, an extreme doctor managed to convince all the doctors and nurses and all of his patients to stop treating themselves. They didn't know that all of the studies she cited were bogus. She wasn't really interested in medicine. She was interested in rhetoric. She had wanted to be an English major, but her family would not pay her tuition for an English degree. No one ever asked to see the studies she referenced. They just trusted she knew the results, and she paraphrased them in such a way that no one contradicted her. She had established authority because she had practiced medicine for over fifty years. Soon the hospital became the place where people came to die and no one was healed there anymore. They closed all the MRI labs, x-rays became a thing of the past, and they ceased treating people for cancer. What no one knew was that this was her plan all along. She liked the idea of tricking everyone; it was like an extended April Fools' joke. You actually believe we shouldn't remove the bullet from that kid's chest? Okay, she thought, if you're all that stupid, we'll just sit here and watch him die while his parents weep and thank me for my trouble. She saved the hospital a bundle, so the administrators were happy. It was one of those cases where someone who was doing a bad thing was believed by everyone to be doing a good thing like when McDonald's commercials feature kids in wheelchairs or single moms.

FISHERMAN'S ITCH

Fisherman's itch occurs when parents don't love each other and stay together for financial reasons and because there are children.

Fisherman's itch is the result of years of alcohol abuse and narcissistic tendencies.

Fisherman's itch involves a lack of empathy.

Fisherman's itch repeats itself from generation to generation.

Fisherman's itch is not something you can scratch.

Fisherman's itch can bring a child to hysteria if she is told it is all in her head.

Fisherman's itch can be easily treated with Benadryl.

Fisherman's itch cannot be relieved if someone would rather enjoy a beer than drive to the drug store.

Fisherman's itch is parasites in polluted water.

BABY KISSING

Baby Kissing is a practice where politicians kiss babies in order to garner public support. This is supposedly the first documented instance of a politician being handed a baby to kiss. I suspect the practice dates back even further. So why on earth are moms so quick to hand over their babies to the least trustworthy people on the planet? I'm talking of course about politicians. We're talking about kissing babies—that revered yet reviled much-analyzed yet meaningless political custom. Nothing says "family values" more than the age-old tactic of politicians posing with kids. A little girl cries as she is placed on the lap of Prime Minister Stephen Harper.

MY CHILDREN

Sometimes I have a dream where I'm giving birth and raising children I don't like and don't have anything in common with. I dream I am sitting at their sporting events or piano lessons or somehow I've convinced them to join Brownies, something my mother could never convince me to do. I dream that I put them in as many activities as I can afford so that I don't have to spend as much time with them. The children I have produced and raised are so draining. All they care about is money and their new boots that look like everyone else's boots. My disinterest in raising my children has resulted in them becoming like everyone else. I try not to show my utter discontent with who and what they have become, and most of them are so self-absorbed they don't even notice—except the girl. I think she knows. I think she can tell.

DON'T DISTURB ME I'M WRITING A LOVE POEM

Don't disturb me I'm writing a love poem
I can't do the dishes I'm writing a love poem
The deadline has passed I'm writing a love poem
I can't finish lunch I'm writing a love poem
Don't hold open the door I'm writing a love poem
I can't go to the protest I'm writing a love poem
I'm at the bus stop I'm writing a love poem
I didn't take a shower I'm writing a love poem
Nobody will get hurt I'm writing a love poem
Don't buy me a lottery ticket I'm writing a love poem
Can you get more paper I'm writing a love poem
My plants are all dead I'm writing a love poem
I've lost every friend I'm writing a love poem
I'm not depressed I'm writing a love poem

WORLD 8

World, if it was just you and me standing at the edge of a cliff, and I could only save one of us, I wouldn't take a moment to even think. I'd give you a little nudge to speed things along as you tumbled all the way down and cracked into pieces. But don't worry. This is a good thing. I'm glad I discovered just how much I despise you. I really feel better about myself now. I feel better about where things stand between us. I would have come to talk to you sooner, but I got busy and then I forgot.

BEE

Did you do everything the bee wanted? Did you stand still and force yourself not to be afraid? Did you let him rest on your collar? Did you let him smell your hair? Were you calm when he nuzzled against your cheek? When he got under your sunglasses, did you let him crawl on your eyelids? And as he walked along your soft, smooth skin, did you remember he was there or did you forget and blink?

BIRDS

—It was a bird fight and some bird tore up another bird's nest that had a bunch of baby birds in it.

—I hope they are not dead.

—Well, they're not fighting over the nest anymore.

—Why not?

—Because they've destroyed it.

NOTES

"Roughing It in the Bush" is an erasure poem created from *Roughing It in the Bush* by Susanna Moodie.

"He Said" in collaboration with Gordon Glendon.

"A Conspiracy to Harm" was part of the Plays Vs. Pipelines protest playwriting relay. Published with permission of the Enpipe Line collective.

"You Look Like a Puppet" comprised of scrambled lines from Joni Mitchell's June 2013 *Q* interview.

ACKNOWLEDGEMENTS

Some poems from this collection have appeared in journals.

"A Bird," *Pilot Pocket Books,* 2015

"April 30 – May 31, 2014," *Advent 2014, Delirious Hem,* December 25, 2014

"Bus Ride," *Pilot Pocket Books,* Issue X, August 23, 2012

"Companion," *Geist,* January 27, 2012

"Sealed Containers," CellStories, mobile publication, 2010

"Sealed Containers," *Lies With Occasional Truth,* online, Winter 2008

THANKS

I'd like to thank the Mansfield Press team—especially Denis De Klerck for being the publisher of one of my favourite presses and including *The Purpose Pitch* among his titles and Stuart Ross for selecting *The Purpose Pitch* for his imprint and for his terrific edits, without which this book would not be this book!

I'd also like to thank my mother, Joyce Mockler, and my sister, Susan Mockler, for their ongoing support and my husband, David Poolman, for reading endless drafts and providing the cover art.

Kathryn Mockler is a poet, fiction writer, and screenwriter. She is the author of *The Saddest Place on Earth* (2012) and *Onion Man* (2011). She is the Toronto editor of *Joyland: a hub for short fiction* and the publisher of the online literary and arts journal *The Rusty Toque*. She teaches creative writing at Western University.

OTHER BOOKS FROM MANSFIELD PRESS

Poetry

Leanne Averbach, *Fever*
Nelson Ball, *In This Thin Rain*
Nelson Ball, *Some Mornings*
Gary Barwin, *Moon Baboon Canoe*
George Bowering, *Teeth: Poems 2006–2011*
Stephen Brockwell, *Complete Surprising Fragments of Improbable Books*
Stephen Brockwell & Stuart Ross, eds., *Rogue Stimulus: The Stephen Harper Holiday Anthology for a Prorogued Parliament*
Diana Fitzgerald Bryden, *Learning Russian*
Alice Burdick, *Flutter*
Alice Burdick, *Holler*
Jason Camlot, *What The World Said*
Margaret Christakos, *wipe.under.a.love*
Pino Coluccio, *First Comes Love*
Marie-Ève Comtois, *My Planet of Kites*
Dani Couture, *YAW*
Gary Michael Dault, *The Milk of Birds*
Frank Davey, *Poems Suitable to Current Material Conditions*
Pier Giorgio Di Cicco, *The Dark Time of Angels*
Pier Giorgio Di Cicco, *Dead Men of the Fifties*
Pier Giorgio Di Cicco, *The Honeymoon Wilderness*
Pier Giorgio Di Cicco, *Living in Paradise*
Pier Giorgio Di Cicco, *Early Works*
Pier Giorgio Di Cicco, *The Visible World*
Salvatore Difalco, *What Happens at Canals*
Christopher Doda, *Aesthetics Lesson*
Christopher Doda, *Among Ruins*
Glen Downie, *Monkey Soap*
Rishma Dunlop, *The Body of My Garden*
Rishma Dunlop, *Lover Through Departure: New and Selected Poems*
Rishma Dunlop, *Metropolis*
Rishma Dunlop & Priscila Uppal, eds., *Red Silk: An Anthology of South Asian Women Poets*
Ollivier Dyens, *The Profane Earth*
Laura Farina, *Some Talk of Being Human*
Jaime Forsythe, *Sympathy Loophole*
Carole Glasser Langille, *Late in a Slow Time*
Suzanne Hancock, *Another Name for Bridge*
Jason Heroux, *Emergency Hallelujah*
Jason Heroux, *Memoirs of an Alias*
Jason Heroux, *Natural Capital*
John B. Lee, *In the Terrible Weather of Guns*
Jeanette Lynes, *The Aging Cheerleader's Alphabet*
David W. McFadden, *Be Calm, Honey*
David W. McFadden, *Shouting Your Name Down the Well: Tankas and Haiku*
David W. McFadden, *What's the Score?*
Leigh Nash, *Goodbye, Ukulele*
Lillian Necakov, *The Bone Broker*
Lillian Necakov, *Hooligans*
Peter Norman, *At the Gates of the Theme Park*
Peter Norman, *Water Damage*
Natasha Nuhanovic, *Stray Dog Embassy*
Catherine Owen & Joe Rosenblatt, with Karen Moe, *Dog*
Corrado Paina, *The Alphabet of the Traveler*
Corrado Paina, *Cinematic Taxi*
Corrado Paina, *The Dowry of Education*
Corrado Paina, *Hoarse Legend*
Corrado Paina, *Souls in Plain Clothes*
Stuart Ross et al., *Our Days in Vaudeville*
Matt Santateresa. *A Beggar's Loom*
Matt Santateresa, *Icarus Redux*
Ann Shin, *The Last Thing Standing*
Jim Smith, *Back Off, Assassin! New and Selected Poems*
Jim Smith, *Happy Birthday, Nicanor Parra*
Robert Earl Stewart, *Campfire Radio Rhapsody*
Robert Earl Stewart, *Something Burned on the Southern Border*
Carey Toane, *The Crystal Palace*
Aaron Tucker, *Punchlines*
Priscila Uppal, *Summer Sport: Poems*
Priscila Uppal, *Winter Sport: Poems*
Steve Venright, *Floors of Enduring Beauty*
Brian Wickers, *Stations of the Lost*

Fiction

Marianne Apostolides, *The Lucky Child*
Sarah Dearing, *The Art of Sufficient Conclusions*
Denis De Klerck, ed., *Particle & Wave: A Mansfield Omnibus of Electro-Magnetic Fiction*
Paula Eisenstein, *Flip Turn*
Sara Heinonen, *Dear Leaves, I Miss You All*
Christine Miscione, *Carafola*
Marko Sijan, *Mongrel*
Tom Walmsley, *Dog Eat Rat*

Non-Fiction

George Bowering, *How I Wrote Certain of My Books*
Denis De Klerck & Corrado Paina, eds., *College Street–Little Italy: Toronto's Renaissance Strip*
Pier Giorgio Di Cicco, *Municipal Mind: Manifestos for the Creative City*
Amy Lavender Harris, *Imagining Toronto*
David W. McFadden, *Mother Died Last Summer*
Deborah Verginella, ed., *Bon Appetito Toronto!*

To order these books, please visit mansfieldpress.net